P9-CAU-580

Metro Litho
Oak Forest, IL 60452

	DATE DUE		

956
BAI

Bailey, Donna
Israel

HUNTLEY CON. SCHOOL
MEDIA CENTER
HUNTLEY, IL 60142

Creek School
Media Center
10   0 Reed Road
Lake in the Hills, IL 60156

Where We Live

Israel

Donna Bailey and Anna Sproule

STECK-VAUGHN
L I B R A R Y
A Division of Steck-Vaughn Company

HUNTLEY CON. SCHOOL
MEDIA CENTER
HUNTLEY, IL 60142

Hello! My name is Shimon, and
this is my sister Ruth.
We live in Israel on a kibbutz.
A kibbutz is a large farm where
many families live and work together.

All the children on our kibbutz
live together in one house.
Our housemother takes care of us
while our parents are at work.
We have to work, too, weeding the garden
outside the house.

After school we help with
the farm work.
We take care of the ducks and geese.
We find food for them to eat.

The babies spend the day in a nursery.
Their mothers drop them off at the nursery
on their way to work.
The housemother takes care of them.

In the evening when the work is done,
we meet our parents and
walk together around the kibbutz.

We grow many different crops
on the kibbutz.
Dad is showing me cotton plants
growing in the field.

It is very hot and dry in
this part of Israel.
In some places we have to lay pipes on
the sandy soil of the desert.
We pump water through the pipes
to water the crops.

We grow some crops inside
plastic greenhouses to help save water.
The plastic traps the water
inside the greenhouse, so
the soil does not dry out.

We grow fruit and vegetables
on the kibbutz, as well as cotton.
Everything grows well with
plenty of water.

Everybody helps pick the vegetables
when they are ready.
In this picture, we are picking
green peppers.
We pack them in boxes to send
to the cities or to other countries.

We sell many vegetables
in the local market, too.
You can buy all sorts of different
fruits and vegetables there.
These women are selling peaches that
were grown near the Dead Sea.

It is very hot by the Dead Sea.
In July, the temperature there
can reach over 92 degrees.
The people there grow oranges which
they send to other countries.

The Dead Sea is very salty because
the hot sun dries up the water.
Where the water is very shallow,
you can see the salt on the ground
by the shore.

Because the sea is so salty,
you stay afloat, even if you can't swim.
Tourists like to go there for fun.
Some even read newspapers while
they are floating!

Other people cover themselves with
thick, black mud from the Dead Sea.
They hope it will make them feel better.
I'd rather swim!

16

In Israel we have many
holidays and festivals.
One of the more important festivals on
the kibbutz is the festival of Shavuot.
Long ago, people used to call it
the Festival of the Wheat Harvest.

HUNTLEY CON. SCHOOL
MEDIA CENTER
HUNTLEY, IL 60142

The festival of Shavuot takes place
in May or June, when the wheat is ripe.
It reminds us of the time when we
believe God gave the people of Israel
the laws Jews try to follow.

For the festival, people build
a harvest shrine in the field
out of bales of straw.
Then they build a platform and
decorate it with leaves and
baskets of flowers.

19

On the day of the festival, men
dress up in white robes and wear
garlands of leaves on their heads.
They stand on the platform, and
a young boy reads a story from the Bible
about the harvest.

One by one,
women and their babies
come up to the platform.
The men give flowers to
the mothers and babies.

Then children come to the platform.
The men give them baskets of flowers
to decorate the harvest shrine.

These boys have many flowers
to put on the shrine.
The flowers remind us of
the Bible story of Moses.
Long ago, God gave Moses
laws for the Jews.

The boys carry flowers to the shrine.
Can you see all the baskets the children
have put at the bottom of the shrine?

Now everyone goes to watch the last field
of wheat being harvested.

Even this tractor has been decorated
with a palm leaf.
The driver checks that a trailer
is hooked to the back of his tractor.

The last field of wheat is cut and
put in bales by the combine harvester.
The tractor follows along with
the harvester, and the men load the bales
onto the trailer.

Now another tractor plows
a long strip of ground where
the wheat has been cut.

Everybody gets a handful of wheat
from the trailer.
They scatter the grain in
the freshly plowed earth.
They hope that next year's harvest
will be a good one, too.

When all the wheat has been cut,
everyone helps decorate the trailers
with leaves.
Then the tractors take the bales of wheat
back to the barns.

This little boy is tired, so
his grandfather gives him a ride
on his horse.
They will follow the tractors
back to the farm.

In the evening everyone gets together
to talk about the day.
They have all enjoyed the fun of
the festival of Shavuot.

Index

Reading Consultant: Diana Bentley
Editorial Consultant: Donna Bailey
Supervising Editor: Kathleen Fitzgibbon

Illustrated by Anna Dzierzek/John Martin and Artists Ltd
Picture research by Suzanne Williams
Designed by Richard Garratt Design

Photographs:
Cover: Tropix/V. J. Birley
Aspect Picture Library: 1 and 12 (Peter Carmichael)
Susan Griggs Picture Agency: 4 (Ted Spiegel), 6 and 9 (Nathan Benn),
    8, 10 and 11 (Tor Eigland)
The Hutchison Library: 2, 3, 5, 7, 16, 23 and 24 (N. D. McKenna)
Tropix: 17, 20, 21, 22, 25, 26, 27, 28, 29, 30, 31 and 32 (Martin Birley)
ZEFA: 13

Library of Congress Cataloging-in-Publication Data: Bailey, Donna. Israel/Donna Bailey and Anna Sproule. p. cm.—
(Where we live) SUMMARY: Depicts the occupations, daily activities, festivals, and ceremonies of Israel. ISBN 0-8114-2558-4
1. Israel—Social life and customs—Juvenile literature. [1. Israel—Social life and customs.] I. Sproule, Anna. II. Title.
III. Series: Bailey, Donna. Where we live. DS112.B28 1990 956.9405'4—dc20 89-22005 CIP AC

HUNTLEY CON. SCHOOL
MEDIA CENTER
HUNTLEY, IL 60142

Copyright © 1990 National Education Corporation
Original copyright © Macmillan Education 1989
All rights reserved. No part of the material protected by this copyright may be reproduced or utilized in any
form or by any means, electronic or mechanical, including photocopying, recording, or by any information
storage and retrieval system, without permission in writing from the copyright owner. Requests for permission
to make copies of any part of the work should be mailed to: Copyright Permissions, Steck-Vaughn Company,
P.O. Box 26015, Austin, Texas 78755. Printed in the United States of America.

1 2 3 4 5 6 7 8 9 LB 96 95 94 93 92 91 90